HILLSIDE PUBLIC LIBRARY

W9-BCY-490

3 1992 00229 0287

JAN 08 2020

HILLSIDE PUBLIC LIBRARY
405 N. HILLSIDE AVENUE
HILLSIDE, IL 60162
708-449-7510

Equal Access
Fighting for Disability Protections™

Disabilities, Sexual Health, and Consent

Ace Ratcliff

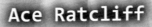

Rosen
YA™

New York

Hillside Public Library

This book is for all disabled humans. I'm fighting every day to make it better for all of us. It's also for Derek, my favorite and best beta reader. Thank you for fighting beside me.

Published in 2020 by The Rosen Publishing Group, Inc.
29 East 21st Street, New York, NY 10010

Copyright © 2020 by The Rosen Publishing Group, Inc.

First Edition

All rights reserved. No part of this book may be reproduced in any form without permission in writing from the publisher, except by a reviewer.

Library of Congress Cataloging-in-Publication Data

Names: Ratcliff, Ace, author.
Title: Disabilities, sexual health, and consent / Ace Ratcliff.
Description: First edition. | New York : Rosen YA, 2020. | Series: Equal access: fighting for disability protections | Includes bibliographical references and index.
Identifiers: LCCN 2018009229| ISBN 9781508183372 (library bound) | ISBN 9781508185918 (pbk.)
Subjects: LCSH: Sex instruction for teenagers. | Sex instruction for people with disabilities—Juvenile literature.
Classification: LCC HQ35 .R38 2016 | DDC 613.9/51087—dc23
LC record available at https://lccn.loc.gov/2018009229

Manufactured in the United States of America

The editors of this resource have consulted various organizations' style guides, including that of the National Center on Disability and Journalism, to ensure the language herein is accurate, sensitive, and respectful. In accordance with NCDJ's recommendation, we have deferred to our author's preference of either people-first or identity-first language.

For some of the images in this book, the people photographed are models and the depictions do not imply actual situations or events.

Contents

Introduction

Sex.

It's a loaded word, isn't it? Maybe you feel uncomfortable just reading it, much less saying it out loud. Or maybe you feel like you know every-thing there is to know about sex. Sometimes it feels like sex is everywhere we look: in our movies, music, television, books, newspapers, and espe-cially online.

As a teenager, it's hard to ignore that sex and sexuality are a huge part of how your body and brain are changing. In fact, a 2011 report by the Centers for Disease Control and Prevention (CDC) found that almost one in two high school students have had sex before graduating, and almost one in five high school students have had four or more partners. Despite this, only twenty-four states (and the District of Columbia) require public schools to incorporate sex education into their regular curricu-lum. Although the CDC recommends sixteen topics as essential components of sex education, including how to create and sustain healthy and respectful relationships and the benefits of being sexually abstinent, fewer than half of high schools and only one-fifth of middle schools teach all of those topics to their students.

While these statistics usually apply to the student body as a whole, it's clear to see that sex edu-cation in the United States is far from satisfactory.

Entertainment such as movies and books regularly feature sex as the main event. This movie poster for *The Notebook* is no exception.

Unfortunately, there aren't many statistics about how disabled students across the nation receive *any* sex education, much less the comprehensive sex education all students deserve. Statistical erasure isn't surprising. Before the adoption of the Americans with Disabilities Act (ADA) in 1990, disabled individuals were far more likely to be denied rights and access to public spaces than they are today. The early and mid-twentieth century found many disabled people institutionalized—or worse—simply because they were disabled. Nondisabled society is just now beginning to understand the

Although one in ten teens or preteens has a disability, disabled people are frequently removed from conversations about sex and sexuality.

6

importance of accessibility and inclusion as disabled people continue to fight for their civil rights.

As a result of the historical exclusion of disabled people, sex and sexuality are infrequently discussed within the spectrum of disability. Based on misinformation or inaccurate stereotypes, society as a whole often assumes that disabled people either have no interest in sex or are incapable of having sex as a result of their disabilities. Even today, disabled teens are sometimes removed or prevented from attending sex education classes with their nondisabled classmates, despite the fact that they are at a much higher risk for sexual assault and rape than the nondisabled population.

However, one in ten teens or preteens has a disability, which is just under 10 percent of the US population aged five to seventeen. Being disabled doesn't erase a person's sexuality, urges, or ability to consent to and have all kinds of sex. As a disabled teen, it's more than your right to have access to comprehensive sex education. It's your responsibility to yourself, your health, and your future partners, should you choose to have them.

Chapter One

The History of Disability and Sexuality

I f you're reading this book, you've definitely heard the word "disabled" at some point. It might be a word someone has used to describe you; it might be a word you use to describe yourself; it might be a word you've only seen listed in a medical chart. Like people, disability comes in all shapes and sizes. Sometimes the word can feel negative or neutral, but it's becoming more common for people to feel a sense of pride when identifying as disabled.

Describing Disability

There are lots of different definitions out there to help you to figure out what "disability" means. The *Merriam-Webster* dictionary defines "disability" as "a ... condition that impairs or limits ... a person's ability to engage in daily activities or interactions." The dictionary's definition reflects an idea called the medical model of disability. Under the medical model, a person's disability is linked to a diagnosis from their doctor. The medical model usually focuses on trying to find a cure for disability, even if that disability is not directly causing harm or pain to the disabled person.

The medical model may remind you of a time in your life when you haven't been able to do something as a result of being disabled—maybe you couldn't go somewhere with your friends because there were stairs to get into the building but no ramp for you to use. Maybe you wanted to go see a movie but there were no showings with captions to allow you to see what the actors were saying. According to the medical model, being disabled is part of the reason why you may not have been

Many nondisabled people understand the idea of medicine helping to correct a disability. Fewer people are comfortable accepting disabilities as normal variations.

able to participate in the same things as your non-disabled friends. The medical model wants to "fix" disabilities, by trying to cure paralysis so people don't have to use wheelchairs or fixing deafness so that everyone can hear what is being said instead of relying on captions.

But learning how to walk isn't really the solution to an inaccessible building. And surgically "curing" deafness can't be the easiest fix for not being able to hear actors. It would be much more feasible for the building to install a ramp that someone could wheel up or for the movie theater to make sure that a deaf person can have access to a device that allows her to read closed captions to understand the movie.

Sign language and hearing aids are two accessible options for making sure deaf and hard of hearing people are included in everyday life.

The social model of disability says that disability is caused by the way society organizes to exclude disabled people, not by whatever your differences are from nondisabled people. The social model of disability is focused on removing barriers that make it so disabled people can't access all the same options as nondisabled people. These barriers may be physical, such as a staircase without a ramp, or they may be social, such as someone saying that installing a ramp is too much work or asking for extra favors. By removing these barriers, disabled people can be independent and equal in society, with access to the same opportunities and experiences that nondisabled people have.

When disabled people have access to wheelchairs, ramps, and other accommodations, it is easier for them to participate in many of the same activities that nondisabled people enjoy.

Historical Erasure

Historically, there are a number of reasons why the medical model has been the main definition of disability for a

11

Identity First or Person First?

When talking about disability, people usually choose between two descriptors: identity-first language (IFL) or person-first language (PFL).

IFL means you put the disability first when describing a person ("disabled person" or "autistic person"). Many people who use IFL believe that their disability is an integral part of who they are and their life experience. They take pride in their identity as a disabled person.

PFL means you put the person first in the description ("person with a disability" or "person with autism"). Many people who use PFL say that they want to be seen as a person first or that they don't want to be defined by their disability. Some people find PFL to be more respectful.

This book uses IFL as the preferred method to further the social model of disability, but you should always ask someone whether they prefer IFL or PFL before assuming or deciding for them.

long time. The eighteenth and nineteenth centuries brought major advances in medicine. These advances led to the idea that the human body became something to be studied, manipulated, and surgically changed.

In the late nineteenth century, a statistician named Francis Galton decided to apply Charles Darwin's theories to people. Galton believed that desirable, "positive" traits (like intelligence or a love of poetry) could be passed on if people who had those traits reproduced, and he believed that undesirable, "negative" traits (such as being a criminal) could be removed from the gene pool if people displaying those negative traits weren't allowed to reproduce. He called this science eugenics.

Eugenics quickly spread across the United States. Disabled people were quickly targeted by eugenicists. Eugenicists began to link disability to undesirable traits such as criminality. At the time, "undesirable" described not only disabled people but also many women, people of color, and people who did not behave in ways

Francis Galton invented the science of eugenics, which negatively influenced the way the world viewed disabled people. That belief system still affects how the disabled community is perceived.

that were deemed socially acceptable. Eugenicists believed that the only way to remove these negative traits from the general population was to prevent disabled people—and other undesirables—from reproducing.

As a result, all fifty US states went on to pass compulsory sterilization laws. These laws specifically targeted disabled people, especially those who were deaf, were blind, or had physical disabilities. These laws made it mandatory for people who were not deemed normal to undergo forced surgery that altered their reproductive organs so that they could not reproduce. Many of these laws were not repealed until the late twentieth century. Unfortunately, according to a 2014 article by Hunter Schwarz in the *Washington Post*, forced sterilizations were even being performed on female inmates in California as late as 2010, and these laws are frequently still in use for some disabled people around the world. In fact, the 1927 US Supreme Court case *Buck v. Bell*, which set a legal standard for the forcible sterilization of intellectually disabled people, has never actually been overturned.

Throughout history, disabled people have been forcibly segregated not only from society but also from healthy, normal sexual activity and reproduction. Disabled people have become scapegoats for undesirable behavior, though scientific connections between the two have been disproved. This history has led to a modern-day assumption that the medical model of disability is the only way to look at disability. It has also contributed to the mis-understanding that disabled people shouldn't—or can't—have sexual desires, needs, or relationships just like everyone else. It's time to bring the social model to sex education for disabled teens, who deserve appropriate, comprehensive sex education instead of outdated, unscientific, and discriminatory stigma.

Myths & Facts

Myth: Disabled people don't need sex education because they won't understand it.

Fact: Being disabled does not necessarily imply that someone's intellectual capabilities are altered. However, even people with intellectual disabilities have sexual relationships. They deserve and need to have sex education for the same reasons everyone else does.

Myth: Disabled people can't have sex.

Fact: Regardless of disability, disabled people are still sexual beings. Some disabled people may not be able to participate in certain types of sex because of their disability, but they can enjoy consensual sexual relationships just like anyone else.

Myth: Disabled people should not be able to have sex, reproduce, and pass on their disability.

Fact: Not all disabilities are hereditary, but even if a disability is inherited, it's not society's job to decide who can have consensual sex and reproduce.

Chapter Two

Biology and the Body

Your body can be a confusing place as you head into puberty. It may seem like there's not enough information for you to figure out the changes you're going through, and even less information that's specifically geared toward how puberty affects a disabled body. Part of what makes figuring this all out even more complex is how unique disabilities can be. A disability may be visible or invisible. A disability may be a mental illness, like bipolar disorder, or it may be a cognitive disorder, like a traumatic brain injury. A person's disability might mean they have to use a wheelchair one day, a cane the next, and no accessibility device at all on another day. Bodies are as unique and individual as disabilities are.

When we talk about sex and sexuality, we often start by talking about our anatomical reproductive systems. Having a basic understanding of your sex organs is important for understanding consent, which is the agreement between people to engage in sexual activity. Sexual activity can encompass many different actions. Knowing more about your body will help you set your own boundaries and navigate what you're comfortable with when it comes

Being honest with yourself and others when discussing your feelings about sex and sexuality leads to much healthier relationships.

to letting another person touch you.

The Female Reproductive System

Our sex organs include our external genitals as well as our internal organs. Although there are some basic assumptions about reproductive organs, everyone's anatomy is different. Your anatomy may be even more unique as a result of your disability. When you were born, a doctor may have assigned you biologically male or female, based on your sex anatomy. The sex you were assigned may not necessarily coincide with your gender identity.

Sexual anatomy that's typically called female includes external and internal reproductive organs. Typically, descriptions of reproductive organs focus specifically on genitals, which are the organs that are used specifically for sex and reproduction. Breasts are not specifically used for the act of reproduction, but they are two mammary glands located on the upper chest, frequently associated with sex and sexuality in Western cultures, so they can be included as an external sex organ.

"Vulva" is the word used to describe the other external sex organs. The vulva is actually one word that describes multiple different body parts. No two vulvae look the same, and puberty may change the way your vulva looks. Above the vulva is the mons pubis, a soft mound of fatty tissue that protects the pubic bone. After puberty begins, pubic hair grows here, which may be something you've already noticed changing in your body. Below the mons pubis are the labia, the folds of skin around the vaginal opening. The labia majora are also covered with pubic hair. The labia minora are inside the outer labia. *Labia* means "lip" in Latin, so you will sometimes hear the labia majora called the outer lips and the labia minora called the inner lips. The skin of the labia may have different colors, textures, or lengths as labia are unique to you.

At the tip of the vulva, where the inner lips meet, is the clitoris. Like labia, the clitoris can vary in size and texture. Usually all you can see of your clitoris is the tip; the rest of the clitoris is inside your body. The clitoris has thousands of nerve endings and is one of the most sensitive parts of the body. Just below the clitoris is a tiny hole called the urethral opening, which is where urine comes out of the body, and just below that is the vaginal opening. The vaginal opening leads to the internal organs of the reproductive system. Sometimes people say "vagina" when they really mean "vulva," which is why it's so important to have an understanding of your body's anatomy.

Mons pubis

Prepuce

Clitoris

Labia majora

Urethral opening

Labia minora

Vaginal opening

Perineal raphe

Anus

If a vagina or vulva is part of your reproductive organs, you can use a mirror to get a detailed look at those parts of your anatomy.

The internal organs of the reproductive system include the vagina, the cervix, and the uterus, which is sometimes also called the womb. Attached to the uterus are the fallopian tubes and the ovaries. These internal reproductive organs make up a complex system that is involved with both the menstrual cycle and pregnancy.

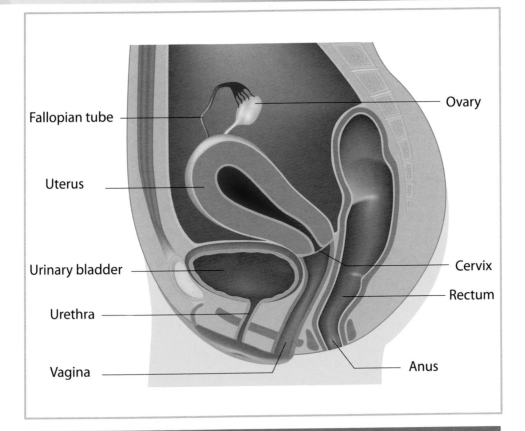

Fallopian tube

Uterus

Urinary bladder

Urethra

Vagina

Ovary

Cervix

Rectum

Anus

The reproductive system is complex, but being familiar with how it functions is vital if you want to understand the full scope of your sexuality.

The Male Reproductive System

Sexual anatomy that's typically called male includes external and internal reproductive organs. Your external reproductive organs are your penis and scrotum. Like the vulva, the penis has different parts, and no two penises look exactly the same. Some penises are curved, while others are

What Should I Call My Reproductive Organs?

Many people are embarrassed to talk about puberty, sex, and reproductive organs. You may have heard people use euphemisms to talk about the human body. People usually use euphemisms because they're uncomfortable. Here are five euphemisms you may have heard and what they actually mean:

Aunt Flo: menstruation or period

Twig-n-berries: the penis and testicles

Naughty bits: genitals

Private parts: penis or vagina

The birds and the bees: the basic facts about sex and sexual intercourse

You should never feel flustered when using accurate words to describe your anatomy. There's no reason to feel ashamed when you're informed about your sexual health and reproductive organs.

straighter. No one should ever feel ashamed about the way their anatomy looks.

While penises may look different, they have the same parts. The end of the penis is called the glans or head. For many people, this is the most sensitive part of the penis. The opening of the urethra is on the glans. This opening is where urine, preejaculate, and semen come from. Preejaculate is a clear, colorless fluid emitted during sexual arousal before ejaculation. Semen is an organic fluid that usually contains sperm, which fertilizes the egg during the reproductive process. Your glans may or may not be covered and protected by a patch of skin called the foreskin. In some cultures, the foreskin is surgically removed very shortly after birth in a surgical process called circumcision, which is why some people have a foreskin and others don't. The frenulum is a V-shaped elastic band of tissue under the glans, where the foreskin meets the underside of your penis. The frenulum can also be very sensitive. It helps contract and retract the foreskin over the glans and is sometimes altered or removed during the circumcision process.

The glans is connected to the shaft of the penis, which extends from the tip to where it connects on your lower abdomen. The penis is made of layers of spongy tissue. Before and during sex, these spongy layers fill with blood, which causes your penis to become hard or erect.

Below your penis is your scrotum, a sack of skin that holds your testicles. Your testicles are glands that make hormones, such as testosterone, and sperm. Another word for testicles is "testes." Your scrotum may be big or small, covered in hair or smooth. Much like vulvae, scrotums are extremely unique to each person.

Inside your scrotum are your internal reproductive organs. These include your epididymis, vas deferens, seminal vesicles, prostate gland, and Cowper's glands. These internal reproductive

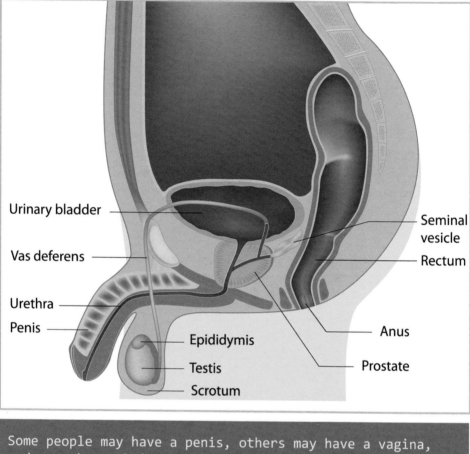

Urinary bladder

Vas deferens

Urethra

Penis

Epididymis

Testis

Scrotum

Seminal vesicle

Rectum

Anus

Prostate

Some people may have a penis, others may have a vagina, and some have their own unique anatomy. It is important to embrace all parts of your sexuality.

organs are involved in the processes of reproduction and sexual pleasure.

Your disability may alter or completely change your anatomy and how you approach sex. You may not have all of the internal or external organs described here. Some people's bodies have a mix of male and female anatomy, either internally or externally. This is known as being an intersex person. You

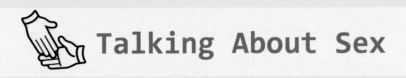

Talking About Sex

Talking openly about sex and reproductive organs can sometimes feel totally cringeworthy, especially when it's a conversation with your parents or another adult. The best way to become comfortable is by practicing. You can start by writing down the words that you're most uncomfortable saying. Say them inside your head over and over until they start feeling normal, maybe even boring. Then practice looking at yourself in the mirror and saying it. Repetition is the key to normalizing something: the more you do it, the more normal it becomes. Eventually, you'll be able to move on to conversations with other people. And because it feels normal to you, you'll probably make the person you're talking to feel more comfortable being open, too.

may have had surgeries or medical interventions that have changed your body, or you may take daily medications that affect your anatomy. Being different is OK. Just remember that understanding your sex organs remains integral to setting limitations and boundaries for how you interact with other people when it comes to sexual activity.

Chapter Three

Sex and Sexuality Are a Spectrum

There are a lot of things to learn about sex and sexuality beside anatomy. One of the most important things to remember is that sex and sexuality are dynamic and fluid; the way you feel about it now may not be the same way you feel ten years from now, even if it is hard to imagine what life will be like in ten years.

As a disabled teen, one of the most challenging parts of learning about sex and sexuality is the pervasive idea that being disabled means sex isn't an option. We are surrounded by advertising that constantly sells us an idealized version of sexiness. Unfortunately, disability is frequently excluded from that idea, even though disabled people make up the largest minority group on the planet. Having any kind of disability is too often shown as something that should be considered shameful or abnormal, but the truth is that disability is just another expression of the amazing variability within the human race. There is nothing inherently unattractive about being disabled. Disabled people can be just as sexy as nondisabled people.

Many nondisabled people are uncomfortable with the idea of disabled people having autonomy regarding sex and sexuality. But disabled people have the right to have consensual sexual relationships just like everyone else.

The Right to Decide

The idea that disabled people should not have sex is very deeply ingrained in our society, in part because of the long history of eugenics. Many people, both disabled and nondisabled, are not even aware that eugenics have played such a large part in how we view disability today. This process of desexualization often means that disabled people are deprived not only of inclusive education about sex and sexuality but also of the experience of satisfying and consensual sexual relationships.

"Sex is something we all want, we all should enjoy, and we all have a right to enjoy," said Mik Scarlet at a TedX talk by Emily Yates called "Undressing Disability." Scarlet is a disabled television actor and a trainer at Enhance the UK, a charity that works to increase sex education and awareness for disabled people in the United Kingdom and across the world. Disability does not preclude sex. As a disabled person, it's important to remember that your sexual desires are natural and normal. Sex can be fun, funny, and OK to enjoy.

Gender and Sexuality

Because disabled people are often eliminated from sex education, they also miss out on basic lessons about gender, gender identity, and sexuality. When you are first beginning to learn about yourself as a sexual being, it can feel overwhelming. Understanding the basics of anatomy is an important first step to learning about sex. Similarly, understanding the basics about gender and sexuality is an important first step in learning about yourself.

Many nondisabled people mistakenly believe that disability is a binary concept: you either use a wheelchair or you don't. But this mind-set excludes many experiences of disability. Similarly, many people believe that sex and gender are binary concepts: that there are only men or women, or that you can only be heterosexual or homosexual. But the truth is that sex, gender, and disability all exist on a spectrum. There are many different ways that all these different parts of yourself can be expressed. You aren't limited to just one option or another.

Understanding Gender Identities

Your biological sex may not necessarily describe your gender or your gender

Much like sexual orientation or gender identity, disability exists on a spectrum and should not be viewed narrowly by nondisabled people.

Sex, sexuality, and gender are individual to each person. Many people express, and even celebrate, their preferences in the way they dress.

identity. Gender and gender identity are usually more complex ideas than the categories of biological sex. Gender is a mix of many different things, including expectations and standards from society about your behaviors and actions. Gender is frequently simplified into male or female and the expectations we have that certain people should act in specific ways. An example is the idea that men should be tough and strong while women should be gentle and empathetic.

Gender identity is more individualistic than gender. Your gender identity is how you feel personally and how you express that feeling. Some people express their gender identity through their clothing or appearance; others use their behavior to express their gender identity. Many people begin to have strong feelings about their gender identity very young, usually around age two or three. Some people don't feel like they fit into the specific category of male or female. These people may choose to describe themselves as genderqueer, genderfluid, or nonbinary.

Some people have an assigned biological sex that matches their gender identity, which means they are cisgender. A person with a penis who identifies as a man is cisgender. A person with a vagina who identifies as a woman is cisgender. Transgender people are those who feel that their gender identity does not match their biological sex.

The Fundamentals of Sex

There are lots of different sexual identities and orientations. Some people learn about their sexual orientation before they start participating in sexual activity; other people may think they identify one way but learn more about themselves as they have sexual experiences. There are many different ways to identify your sexuality, and sexual identification can sometimes overlap with gender identification. You may not feel like you have a complete grip on your gender identity or your sexual identity—and that's OK. Sex really is a constant learning experience.

LGBTQIA+

In the United States before the 1960s, there was no common vocabulary for people who had a sexual identity outside of heterosexuality. Usually the words used to describe people who identified this way were meant as an insult. As mainstream society has become more accepting of the diversity and differences in sexuality and gender identities, the words we use to describe people have also evolved. You may have seen the initialism LGBTQIA+ used to describe gender identity and sexual orientation. The initials represent the following:

- Lesbian: A woman who is sexually and/or romantically attracted to other women.
- Gay: A man who is sexually and/or romantically attracted to other men. Also used generally to refer to same-sex attraction.
- Bisexual: A person who is attracted sexually and/or romantically to both men and women.
- Transgender: A person whose gender identity does not correspond with their biological sex.
- Queer: An umbrella term for sexual and gender minorities who are not heterosexual and/or cisgender.
- Intersex: An umbrella term for a variety of conditions in which a person is born with reproductive or sexual anatomy that does not fit

the standard definitions for male or female.
- Asexual: A person who is not sexually and/or romantically attracted to either men or women.
- +(Plus): An umbrella term used to include other gender or sexual identities that do not fall under the other categories.

While LGBTQIA+ doesn't necessarily include all individuals and subgroups, knowing its meaning will not only help you be a more inclusive person but may also help you understand more about yourself.

Just as there are many variations in the way someone can identify their gender, gender identity, and sexual identity, there are also different ways people can participate in the act of sex itself. Sex comes in many different forms, and people may have different ideas of what constitutes sex. Some people believe that penis-in-vagina (PIV) intercourse is the only kind of sex, but that's not true. Different types of sex include oral sex (mouth to genital contact), anal sex (penis in anus intercourse), and even contact between your hands and genitals or someone else's genitals. You can also learn about sex and what you like or dislike by participating in masturbation, the sexual stimulation of your own genitals.

Having a disability may mean that the act of sex is more complicated or complex. You may need to

Hillside Public Library

Abstinence Is Always an Option

It's important to remember that while there's a lot of pressure out there to become sexually active, it's OK if you don't feel like you're ready to become sexually intimate with anyone. That's a decision that no one else can make but you. It doesn't matter how old you are. If you're not comfortable being sexually active in any way, shape, or form, you don't have to be. One of the nice things about being abstinent is that you know you will be completely avoiding exposure to the negative sides of sex. If you're abstinent and completely refrain from sexual activity, you don't have to deal with issues like pregnancy or sexually transmitted infections. It's OK if you spend your entire life without the desire to be sexually active.

work around assistive devices or adjust the way you participate in sexual activity to suit what works best with your body, but that doesn't mean that you can't have a fulfilling, satisfying, and educated sex life.

You Know Best

Deciding when to have sex and what kind of sexual activity to engage in can be a big deal, and there are some real risks that come along with sex, like

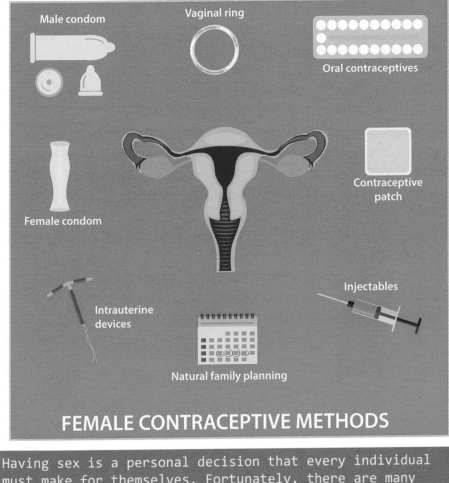

Male condom

Vaginal ring

Oral contraceptives

Contraceptive patch

Female condom

Injectables

Intrauterine devices

Natural family planning

FEMALE CONTRACEPTIVE METHODS

Having sex is a personal decision that every individual must make for themselves. Fortunately, there are many options to help minimize the potential consequences of sexual activity, including pregnancy.

unintended pregnancy or the transmission of diseases or infections. The use of contraceptives or birth control can help prevent negative outcomes from sex. This practice may include condoms, dental dams, intrauterine devices, or hormonal medication. Regular checkups may also be important when you become sexually active. Choosing the right birth control usually means having a conversation with a trusted adult or a doctor. While conversations like this may feel awkward or uncomfortable, protecting your health now will be something that benefits you for the rest of your life.

You know your body best. You know yourself better than all of your doctors and even your parents because you live in your body every single day. The decisions you make about your gender identity, your sexual identity, and your sexual activity are all important because of how they affect you both physically and emotionally. At the end of the day, you're the most important part of the equation. It's vital that you trust your instincts when it comes to these important issues.

Chapter Four

The Best Sex Is Collaborative Sex

One of the most important decisions to make about sex—any kind of sex—is whether it's something you're comfortable participating in. If and when you make the decision that you want to move forward in a sexual experience with another person or people, you're going to need to understand the idea of consent. Consent is the most important part of a sexual encounter, whether sex is a single experience or a long-term relationship with multiple interactions.

Cornerstones of Consent

Consent is an agreement between two people to engage in activity of some kind. Many people talk about consent specifically within the confines of sex, but consent is an important part of communication in many situations outside of sexual activity. You probably give or ask for consent many times throughout your day. For example, if you're at school and you ask to use the restroom, you've asked for consent. If your teacher said yes, they gave you consent. Asking to share toys with your friends as a little kid is often one of the first experiences you may have had with consent. You may have had a favorite toy that a friend played with without asking for permission. If that friend broke the toy, you probably felt terrible.

Consent is a crucial part of sexual interactions, especially when it comes to bodily autonomy, which is the idea that you have self-determination and self-control over your own body. You have the right to say yes or no in every sexual encounter you have with another person. The best sexual experiences are collaborative sex, which means

The question of consent comes up in many different situations. It can mean something as simple as asking for permission to leave the classroom, but also applies to how one should be treated when engaging in sexual activity.

you and your partner check in regularly with each other to make sure you're doing things that the other person is comfortable with and enjoying.

If and when you get to a point where you have decided you're ready to have a sexual experience with another person, consent should be an ongoing, enthusiastic conversation during the whole experience. The more you practice giving and receiving consent, the easier it will become for you.

Sometimes consent is given verbally, using the words yes or no. Sometimes you or your partner may use different variations of those words. Telling your partner something feels good or asking them to continue doing what they're doing is another way of giving consent. Sometimes consent may be communicated in a nonverbal way by using facial expressions and body language. But it is always safer for everyone involved if consent is communicated clearly and verbally.

Some states have laws in place that govern who

Nonverbal communication like smiling and laughing is one way to communicate that you are interested in starting a romantic relationship with another person.

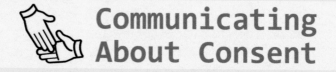

Communicating About Consent

Even in everyday interactions, communication can be difficult. Add sex to the mix and you can feel particularly shy or nervous. Remember, being direct is sometimes the best way to start a conversation about consent. If you don't feel like you can openly communicate with your partner, they might not be the right partner for you. If your partner says no or seems unsure, don't pressure them. Sometimes people feel like they are communicating enough using their body language, but unspoken signals can be extremely challenging to try to interpret. Most important, silence is not consent. Think about how you would feel in a similar situation. Enthusiastic consent is always the sexiest way to be intimate.

can and cannot give consent. In some states, people cannot legally consent to sexual activity of any kind if they are below a certain age, even if the person says that they wanted the sexual activity to take place. Having sex with someone under the age of consent is called statutory rape, which is a crime. Also, if someone is drunk or high on drugs, they cannot give consent. In fact, if a person is intoxicated, even if they seem as though they want to engage in sexual activity, they cannot legally consent. Breaking these laws may be considered sexual assault or rape.

Talk About It

Many people feel shy about repeatedly asking for consent in sexual situations. Checking in with your partner is actually one of the best ways you can build trust. Sometimes being the first one to ask ends up being a good way to help your partner feel comfortable mirroring the same behavior. Checking in with each other will help you respect each other's comfort levels and make the sexual experience more enjoyable and ethical.

Clear communication about consent is impossible when one partner is under the influence of drugs or alcohol. Taking advantage of someone in this position is considered a type of sexual assault.

When giving consent, it's important to remember that you have the right to say no to anyone at any time. You do not have to explain yourself beyond that, no matter what your partner says. It's even OK to change your mind in the middle of a sexual encounter. If you become uncomfortable with something you're doing with another person, you are always allowed to stop. No one has a right to touch you if you don't want to be touched. You have the right to limit access to your body by other people. Since you know how important it is that people listen when you say stop, it's equally as important that you respect when someone else says no.

This right to limit access to your body extends to situations where you are participating in something you've already done with someone before. If

Being able to say no to a sexual experience is a right you always retain, no matter the circumstance. You never have to explain why you don't want to have sex with another person.

you've kissed someone before, but you don't want to kiss them now, you're allowed to communicate that. If you've had sex with someone before, but you don't want to have sex with them now, you are allowed to say no. Sometimes people will even decide on a safe word before any sexual activity. This is a prearranged, clear, and unambiguous word that is used as a signal to end an activity. Safe words can include versions of stop and no. Safe words may also be full phrases or even nonsense words, like "flamingo."

Vulnerability Affects Consent

Sometimes, disability may mean that you are in a more vulnerable position than a nondisabled person, which can make consent more confusing. This vulnerability may be perceived due to disableism, which is discriminatory, oppressive, or abusive behaviors that stem from the idea that disabled people are inferior to nondisabled people.

Because of this vulnerability, you may feel pressure to say yes to intimate experiences or sexual activities. Society can reinforce an ingrained feeling that if someone wants or desires you sexually that you should take what you can get or accept the attention, even if you don't want to. It's important to remember that being disabled does not mean you are undesirable or not sexy. Being disabled also does not mean you are lucky because someone is sexually interested in you. Being disabled doesn't mean you should consent to something you don't want to do. Anyone who pressures you into sexual activity you are not comfortable with is not keeping you safe.

Sometimes, the vulnerability that comes from disability may be a physical reality. If you are paraplegic, you may not have the physical ability to stop someone who is doing something you don't want them to do. You may need to set up a safety plan with a person whom you trust in order to make sure that you are not physically abused or assaulted.

Whether your vulnerability is perceived or real, it may affect your ability to consent to a sexual activity or experience. It's important to remember that you have the same rights to control your body and make decisions that any nondisabled person does, and you are never in the wrong for enacting your rights.

10 Great Questions to Ask a Sex Educator

1. Can someone tell if I'm a virgin or not?

2. Will having sex for the first time hurt?

3. What can I do if I'm being sexually abused?

4. Can guys be raped, too?

5. What is an orgasm?

6. Do people choose to identify as LGBTQIA+?

7. Does having sex mean I'll fall in love?

8. How do I know if my body is sexually healthy?

9. Can you get pregnant the first time you have sex?

10. Does sex feel different with a condom or dental dam?

Chapter Five

Disability and Abuse

Content warning: This chapter will discuss sexual abuse, sexual assault, and rape.

Having a basic understanding of anatomy, sex, sexuality, and gender is important as you become more comfortable with the way you identify and think about the sexual experiences you may or may not want to participate in as you get older. It's important to include disabled people in detailed conversations about sex education because they have some of the highest rates of assault or abuse related to sex or relationships. According to the World Health Organization (WHO), children with disabilities are almost four times more likely to experience violence than nondisabled children. The same WHO report notes that disabled children are almost three times more likely to be victims of sexual violence. Disability Justice, an online resource for those in the legal profession, states that disabled kids are twice as likely to be abused as their nondisabled peers. The abuse they experience is usually more severe, more likely to happen multiple times, and more likely to be repeated over a longer period of time. And according to the US Justice

The "It's on Us" initiative is an awareness campaign focused on ending sexual assualt on campus. In this picture, army personnel wave shirts with the slogan in support of the movement.

Department, there is an 85 percent chance that the abuser will be someone the disabled person knows rather than a stranger.

Without Consent

Any behavior that the victim does not consent to and intentionally harms them or makes them afraid is considered abuse. Abusers force their victims to participate in unwanted acts using different techniques. Sometimes the pressure they use is physical. Someone who is bigger than their victim may block the door, so the victim can't get away or be allowed to move. Perpetrators may try to manipulate or intimidate victims by threatening to hurt them or someone they love. They may rely on emotional coercion to force a victim into nonconsensual sex, perhaps by making the victim feel guilty for not having sex, even if that person is not comfortable with it. Some abusers use a combination of all these techniques to sexually assault their victims. These techniques can be very confusing when the perpetrator is someone you know and especially if they are someone you trust or love.

Abuse that occurs in an intimate relationship between people is called domestic violence or relationship abuse. Disabled people may be abused by their partners, such as their girlfriends or boyfriends. Disabled people may also be abused by their caretakers, family, close friends, or even someone on their medical team. Abusers can take many forms and so can abuse.

Sexual assault or sexual abuse refers to sexual contact or behavior that occurs without the consent of a person, usually referred to as the victim. Sexual assault can take many different forms. Like so many other things related to sex, it can occur along a spectrum. Sexual assault may include someone touching your body without your consent or someone forcing you to participate in sexual acts that you have not consented to performing. Someone touching your breasts without your permission is a type of sexual assault. Someone forcing you to participate in oral sex without your consent is also a type of sexual assault.

Abuse means more than physically assaulting someone by kicking or punching. Emotional abuse is more subtle, but can be just as damaging.

Rape is a specific form of sexual assault, but not all acts of sexual assault are rape. The word "rape" is often used to describe sexual penetration without consent, such as when someone places their body parts or an object into a victim's vagina or anus without the victim's consent.

Different Kinds of Abuse

Sexual assault is not the only kind of abuse that disabled people are likely to experience in their lifetimes. Disabled people may also experience emotional abuse (also known as psychological abuse or verbal abuse), where the perpetrator does not physically harm them but instead inflicts damage that leads to mental trauma, like anxiety or depression. Perpetrators do this by controlling their victims, isolating them from friends or family, or calling them names. Emotional abuse can be hard to recognize, but it is just as damaging as physical abuse. Emotional abuse is extremely manipulative, and it is sometimes difficult to explain how this type of abuse affects you. One of the best ways you can learn to identify emotional abuse is by recognizing how you feel after interacting with someone: Do you feel embarrassed? Humiliated? Hurt? If you have a negative experience every time you interact with someone, you may be experiencing emotional abuse.

Finding Help

Getting help when abuse happens can sometimes be a challenge for disabled victims. Disabled people are sometimes isolated. They may be dependent on a small circle of friends or have a specific group of caretakers. Sometimes they live in a group home that segregates them from other parts of society. In addition, barriers in accessibility frequently make reporting abuse more challenging for disabled people. It would be almost impossible to report a rape at a police station if you were deaf and communicate only in American Sign Language (ASL) and did not have an interpreter to help you talk to a police officer.

Warning Signs of Nontraditional Abuse

While it's not always easy to tell at the beginning of a relationship if it will become abusive, you can learn some common signs that an abuser might be trying to gain power and control over his disabled victim.

Abusers may:

- Damage a victim's assistive device so that they can't go anywhere without help
- Withhold medical care so that the victim becomes sick
- Threaten service or emotional support animals in an attempt to manipulate
- Refuse to take care of the disabled victim so they feel isolated and alone
- Cash disability checks without permission so that the disabled victim does not have financial resources to care for themselves

Many people mistakenly believe that there are certain kinds of people who are more likely to become victims of abuse or that there are clear warning signs at the beginnings of all abusive relationships. Many kinds of abuse are subtler than that, but recognizing early signs is a good first step to learning how to protect yourself.

Many disabled kids will experience some form of trauma or abuse before making the individual choice to become sexually active. Trauma and abuse can affect your sexuality. Sometimes it takes a long time to heal from abuse. If you decide to consent to sexual activity after experiencing abuse, it's important to remember that you deserve a partner who will respect your boundaries and behave in a way that makes you feel safe and secure. Victims are never responsible for someone else's abusive actions.

Abusers often view disabled people as easy targets, and these abusers take advantage of the person's disabilities to get what they want without the victim's consent. Disabled people may have difficulty recognizing when they are experiencing abuse. A cognitive or communication disability may cause the victim to have difficulty recognizing when they are being abused. And some disabled people have no background or understanding of what a normal, healthy, consensual relationship is like because they have never been taught.

The lack of information and education may lead victims to believe that the way they're being treated is normal or that it's something they deserve. Sometimes abusers will take advantage of this lack of information and begin the process of grooming their disabled victims. Grooming is a slow, methodical process of manipulating a victim into trusting the perpetrator before abuse begins.

The fact that disabled people are so vulnerable to assault is an additional reason why they need access to fundamental, thorough sex education. In

Your disability is an important part of who you are, and embracing all aspects of yourself includes expressing what you need and deserve when it comes to sex.

an interview with National Public Radio (NPR) Michael Gill, author of *Already Doing It: Intellectual Disability and Sexual Agency*, stated, "If people know what sexual assault is, they become empowered in what is sexuality and what they want in sexuality."

Feeling empowered and in control of your body is an important part of becoming a sexual being. Learning how to embrace your disability and begin the process of discovering more about yourself is the first step in your journey of learning more about sex, sexuality, and consent.

Glossary

ableism A form of discrimination that views non-disabled people as superior to disabled people.

accessibility The ability for everyone to access, use, and benefit from everything in their environment.

bodily autonomy The belief that a person should have self-determination and self-control over their own body.

circumcision A surgical process often performed shortly after birth to remove the foreskin from the penis.

clitoris A sex organ that has thousands of nerve endings and is one of the most sensitive parts of the body.

eugenics A belief that the human race can be improved by encouraging or discouraging certain populations from reproducing.

euphemism An inoffensive word used as a substitute instead of a more accurate term.

foreskin A patch of skin that covers and protects the glans of the penis.

gender identity A person's sense of their own gender and how they outwardly express their gender of choice.

genderqueer Not subscribing to conventional gender distinctions but identifying with neither, both, or a combination of male and female genders.

identity-first language (IFL) Putting the disability first when describing a person, often as a point of pride.

intersex A person whose body has a mix of male and female anatomy, either internally or externally.

labia The folds of skin around the vaginal opening, including the labia majora and the labia minora.

masturbation The sexual stimulation of your own genitals.

mons pubis A soft mound of fatty tissue that protects the pubic bone where pubic hair grows.

nonbinary Not fitting into the specific category of male or female.

nonconsensual Not mutually agreed upon, often used when referring to an intimate relationship.

perpetrator A person who commits an illegal or immoral act.

psychological abuse Abuse where the perpetrator does not physically harm the victim but inflicts damage that leads to mental trauma, such as anxiety, depression, or post-traumatic stress disorder.

rape A specific form of sexual assault that involves sexual penetration without the other person's consent.

safe word A prearranged, clear, and unambiguous word that is used to signal a desire to end a sexual activity.

statutory rape The act of having sex with someone who is legally underage and cannot consent.

transgender A person whose gender identity does not correspond with their biological sex.

For More Information

Abused Deaf Women's Advocacy Services (ADWAS)
8623 Roosevelt Way NE
Seattle, WA 98115
(206) 922-7088
Website: http://www.adwas.org
Facebook: @ADWAServices
Twitter: @ADWAS1986
ADWAS empowers deaf and deaf-blind survivors of
   domestic violence, sexual assault, and harass-
   ment by providing access to community education, advocacy on policy issues, and comprehensive individual services.

Action Canada for Sexual Health & Rights
251 Bank Street, 2nd Floor
Ottawa, ON K2P 1X3
Canada
(888) 642-2725
Website: https://www.actioncanadashr.org
Facebook and Twitter: @actioncanadaSHR
Action Canada works to ensure that women in Canada and around the world are supported as they
   seek to maintain and advance their sexual health
   and reproductive rights.

Americans with Disabilities Act (ADA) National
   Network
(800) 949-4232
Website: https://adata.org
Facebook: @ADANetwork
Twitter and Instagram: @ADANational

The ADA National Network is committed to providing training and support to state and local gov-
ernment agencies, employers, service providers,
family members, and others invested in the issues
covered by the ADA.

Canadian Foundation for Women's Health (CFWH)
2781 Lancaster Road
Suite 200
Ottawa, ON K1B 1A7
Canada
(613) 730-4192, ext. 254
Website: https://cfwh.org
Facebook: @CFWH.org
Twitter: @BetweenTheHips
CFWH's mission is to improve the reproductive and
sexual health of Canadian women throughout
their lives. The organization supports funding for
research related to women's health issues.

National Violence Domestic Hotline
PO Box 161810
Austin, TX 78716
(800) 799-7233 (voice)
(800) 787-3224 (TTY)
Website: http://www.thehotline.org
Facebook: @NationalDomesticViolenceHotline
Instagram: @ndvhofficial
Twitter: @ndvh
A twenty-four-hour, confidential, toll-free hotline
through which highly trained advocates provide
support, information, planning, and crisis inter-
vention in 170 languages to victims of domestic

violence and relationship abuse.

Planned Parenthood (PP)
123 William Street, 10th Floor
New York, NY 10038
(800) 230-7526
Website: http://www.plannedparenthood.org
Facebook: @PlannedParenthood
Instagram: @plannedparenthood
Twitter: @PPFA
A nonprofit organization that provides health care
    services for women, men, and young peo-
    ple, as well as reproductive health information
    and services.

Rape, Abuse & Incest National Network (RAINN)
1220 L Street NW
Washington, DC 20005
(800) 656-HOPE (4673)
Website: http://www.rainn.org
Facebook: @RAINN01
Twitter and Instagram: @RAINN
The largest nonprofit anti–sexual assault organiza-
    tion in the United States, RAINN works to pre-
    vent sexual assault, support survivors, and make
    sure that perpetrators are brought to justice
    through victim services, public education, public
    policy, and consulting services.

For Further Reading

Bailey, Jacqui. *Sex, Puberty, and All That Stuff: A Guide to Growing Up.* Hauppauge, NY: Barron's, 2016.

Burcaw, Shane. *Not So Different: What You Really Want to Ask About Having a Disability.* New York, NY: Roaring Book Press, 2017.

Coolhart, Deborah, Jayme Peta, and Rylan Jay Testa. *The Gender Quest Workbook: A Guide for Teens and Young Adults Exploring Gender Identity*. Oakland, CA: New Harbinger Publications, 2016.

Corinna, Heather. *S.E.X.: The All-You-Need-to-Know Sexuality Guide to Get You Through Your Teens and Twenties.* Boston, MA: De Capo Lifelong Books, 2016.

Harris, Robie H. *It's Perfectly Normal: Changing Bodies, Growing Up, Sex, and Sexual Health.* Somerville, MA: Candlewick Press, 2014.

Hasler, Nikol. *Sex: An Uncensored Introduction.* San Francisco, CA: Zest Books, 2015.

Henderson, Elisabeth. *100 Questions You'd Never Ask Your Parents: Straight Answers to Teens' Questions About Sex, Sexuality, and Health*. New York, NY: Roaring Book Press, 2014.

Kuklin, Susan. *Beyond Magenta: Transgender Teens Speak Out.* London, UK: Walker Books and Subsidiaries, 2016.

Pardes, Bronwen. *Doing It Right: Making Smart, Safe, and Satisfying Choices About Sex.* New York, NY: Simon Pulse, 2013.

Bibliography

Disability Justice. "Abuse and Exploitation of People with Developmental Disabilities." Retrieved February 2, 2018. http://disabilityjustice.org /justice-denied/abuse-and-exploitation.

Disability Nottinghamshire. "The Social Model vs. the Medical Model of Disability." Retrieved January 22, 2018. http://www .disabilitynottinghamshire.org.uk/about /social-model-vs-medical-model-of-disability.

Gender Spectrum. "Understanding Gender." Retrieved January 23, 2018. https://www .genderspectrum.org/quick-links/understanding -gender.

Henley, Ariel. "Why Sex Education for Disabled People Is So Important." Teen Vogue, October 5, 2017. https://www.teenvogue.com/story /disabled-sex-ed.

National Conference of State Legislatures. "State Policies on Sex Education in Schools." December 21, 2016. http://www.ncsl.org/research/health /state-policies-on-sex-education-in-schools.aspx.

National Domestic Violence Hotline. "Domestic Violence and People with Disabilities." Retrieved February 11, 2018. http://www.thehotline.org /is-this-abuse/domestic-violence-disabilities.

Planned Parenthood. "Sexual and Reproductive Anatomy." Retrieved February 11, 2018. https://www .plannedparenthood.org/learn/health-and-wellness /sexual-and-reproductive-anatomy.

Rape, Abuse, and Incest National Network. "What Consent Looks Like." Retrieved February 16, 2018. https://www.rainn.org/articles/what-is -consent.

Shapiro, Joseph. "For Some with Intellectual Disabilities, Ending Abuse Starts with Sex Ed." National Public Radio, January 9, 2018. https:// www.npr.org/2018/01/09/572929725/for-some -with-intellectual-disabilities-ending-abuse-starts -with-sex-ed.

Smith, S. E. "Disabled People Are Still Being Forcibly Sterilized—So Why Aren't People Talking About It?" Rewire, November 17, 2014. https:// rewire.news/article/2014/11/17/disabled -people-still-forcibly-sterilized-isnt-anyone -talking.

Stern, Alexandra. "That Time the United States Sterilized 60,000 of Its Citizens." Huffington Post, January 7, 2016. https://www.huffingtonpost.com.

UC Davis LGBTQIA Resource Center. "LGBTQIA Resource Center Glossary." Retrieved February 2, 2018. https://lgbtqia.ucdavis.edu/educated /glossary.html.

World Health Organization. "Violence Against Adults and Children with Disabilities." Retrieved March 1, 2018. http://www.who.int/disabilities /violence/en.

Yates, Emily. "Undressing Disability." TedX Talks, April 1, 2016. https://www.youtube.com /watch?v=fkq3cIgVhR8.

Index

About the Author

Ace Ratcliff is a disabled, nonbinary writer, artist, photographer, and model who lives and works in Oakland, California. Much of her work centers on intersectional feminism, with a specific focus on disability justice. She lives with hypermobile Ehlers-Danlos syndrome, dysautonomia, and mast cell activation syndrome, which all make for a particularly rebellious meatcage. She is a former mortician with an associate's degree in funeral services from American River College in Sacramento, California, and a bachelor's degree in political science from the University of Central Florida in Orlando, Florida. She co-owns Harper's Promise, an in-home pet euthanasia, hospice, and palliative care service with her fiancé, Derek. She can almost always be found with a dog by her side.

Photo Credits

Cover, p. 1 Mikael Vaisanen/Corbis/Getty Images; p. 5 AF archive/Alamy Stock Photo; p. 6 Andrey Popov/Shutterstock .com; p. 9 BSIP SA/Alamy Stock Photo; p. 10 ©Will Hart/ PhotoEdit; p. 11 ©Cleo Photography/PhotoEdit; p. 13 Art Collection 2/Alamy Stock Photo; p. 18 Rawpixel/iStock/ Thinkstock; pp. 20, 21, 24 Alila Medical Media/ Shutterstock.com; p. 27 Tim Garcha/Corbis/Getty Images; p. 29 Tuzemka/Shutterstock.com; p. 30 Mike Kemp/Corbis Historical/Getty Images; p. 35 Photoroyalty/Shutterstock .com; p. 38 Huntstock/Thinkstock; p. 39 franckreporter/E+/ Getty Images; p. 41 Fabiana Ponzi/Shutterstock.com; p. 42 Viorel Sima/Shutterstock.com; p. 47 Tim Clayton/Corbis/ Getty Images; p. 49 Dragon Images/Shutterstock.com; p. 53 Westend61/Getty Images.

Design: Tahara Anderson; Editor: Jennifer Landau; Photo Researcher: Sherri Jackson